ACTIVE MATH

Games and activities to help children in pre-school and early grades learn basic mathematical concepts

ADRIAN B. SANFORD

WORLD TEACHERS PRESS®

Printed in the United States of America.

Cover and interior design and production by Rollins Design and Production.

Illustrations for text and cover by Tim Haggerty.

Editorial development by Janet McCartney.

Order Number 2-5086

ISBN 1-58324-008-X

A B C D E F 00 01 02 03 04 05

Didax
Educational Resources

395 Main Street
Rowley, MA 01969
www.worldteacherspress.com

CONTENTS

PREFACE

The study of mathematics offers just one of many possible perceptions of the world, but a beautifully elegant one. When children are allowed free play time, mathematical games often spring up by virtue of the children's own imaginations. When I see this happening, I am further convinced that games and activities are fundamental to teaching mathematics to youngsters. At the very least, the sheer pleasure that children derive from these games reaffirms their effectiveness.

The following is a discussion of some of the enjoyable ways children can learn the basics of mathematics and the many ways that their caregivers, teachers, and parents, can guide them in the process.

CHILDREN'S PERCEPTION OF MATH

Adults perceive math differently from children. Mathematics, after all, is a structured and patterned way of seeing the world. Adults see patterns and know processes that are hidden from children. Our aim as parents and teachers is to reveal these patterns and processes so that our children will become math literate. We must be aware of children's perceptions and learning styles in order to aid them in that process.

Children learn about the world of mathematics in the same way that humankind has learned it from the beginning of time. One can imagine a prehistoric family with a herd of goats using pebbles to represent them, one for one. How many goats do we have? Count the pebbles. Pebbles-for-goats becomes an efficient counting process.

As civilizations evolved, cultures developed language and rudimentary markings. They could keep track of common objects, like livestock, with words and symbols. Eventually, the markings became numbers, which became the cornerstone of mathematics. Numbering is a conceptual system of representation, a useful abstraction we carry in our minds when the actual objects are not visible. For example, by assigning numbers, we would know that the number of objects one possesses is seven, even if the objects are not within sight. In this way, the symbols of math, or numbers, foster memory, mobility, and communication.

To explore and learn about the world of mathematics, its symbols and processes, children first need an affirmation of their own experiences and what their senses tell them. This premise, clearly articulated by Froebel, Pestalozzi, Montessori, Piaget, and others—has been widely accepted for generations. In order to learn, children require active involvement in seeing, touching, and manipulating the things that the symbols of mathematics represent. They require that mathematics be presented in a way that they can understand it, which is active mathematics.

CHILDREN LEARN MATH THROUGH THEIR SENSES

As they are learning, children require a wide variety of sensory experiences from which they can build their own abstractions. They gain a sense of structure and quantity through touching as well as seeing and hearing. They gain a sense of distance by moving from one place to another, a sense of height by stacking objects. Through sensory perceptions they solidify concepts. Active Math poses questions to children. Many questions arise naturally out of their experience. For example, How many blocks are in the bag? How many groups can be made? Which tower is taller? Which wall has more blocks? Which is longer? What is the shortest way to get from Point A to Point B?

Active Math offers game-like experiences with manipulative materials, including children's own bodies. These games invite children to move playfully from the real to the symbolic—at their own best learning pace. This integration of learning with play fuels children's natural curiosity about mathematical patterns and structures, and is the primary teaching philosophy of **Active Math.**

CHILDREN DISCOVER THE BASICS OF MATH

To grow in mathematics, children need to learn the basic operations of arithmetic: counting, grouping, adding, subtracting, multiplying and dividing. They do this best by actively (physically) engaging in the operations.

They begin with counting.

- **Counting** is keeping track of things, like fingers, or steps taken.

- **Grouping** is lumping things together, which often makes counting easier. Having five fingers on each hand makes it easier to count to ten.

- **Adding** is counting, as in counting fingers, or counting a first group of steps, say, and then counting the next group of steps to see how many it takes altogether to reach a new point. Children discover how the process of adding grows naturally out of counting and grouping.

- **Subtracting** is taking steps back from that new point—stepping backward as it were—and then counting how many backward steps you took. Again, counting underlies the process of subtraction.

- **Multiplying** is jumping ahead by long, even leaps over equal groups of small steps (two, three, or more) in each leap, and repeatedly adding the number of small steps covered by each leap.

- **Dividing** is counting how many long, even leaps, you must take to get from the original point to the end point.

This is **Active Math.** (Otherwise known as "Grandpa Adrian's Math Games for Grand Children.")

NCTM STANDARDS

Each activity is cross referenced to the NCTM standards for grades K–4. These standards are the skills and concepts recommended by the National Council of Teachers of Mathematics as fundamental components of the curriculum. A complete description of the standards is available in book format from: NCTM, Inc., 1906 Association Drive, Reston, VA 22091.

The focus of the standards are as follows:

Standard 1:	Mathematics as problem solving
Standard 2:	Mathematics as communication
Standard 3:	Mathematics as reasoning
Standard 4:	Mathematical connections
Standard 5:	Estimation
Standard 6:	Number sense and numeration
Standard 7:	Concepts of whole number operations
Standard 8:	Whole number computation
Standard 9:	Geometry and spatial sense
Standard 10:	Measurement
Standard 11:	Statistics and probability
Standard 12:	Fractions and decimals
Standard 13:	Patterns and relationships

Many of the games collected here call for a leader to get things started. The leader may be a teacher or any other caregiver, such as a parent. When a child becomes familiar with the way a particular game is played, he or she may become the leader.

As children are completing the activities, it is critical that each child feel a sense of accomplishment. Many young children become tense when competing against each other. Therefore, it is recommended that the leader assist each child in setting his or her own performance level at the beginning of each activity. The child's goal would then be to improve his or her performance level. Instead of playing against each other, they will then play against (and for) themselves.

Every child a winner!

Every child a learner!

— Adrian B. Sanford

ACKNOWLEDGMENTS

Active Math is a collection of simple but effective math games, which have evolved out of my experiences with my own children and grandchildren and, in the past decade, with children and their caregivers at several educational institutions.

I would like to acknowledge the thoughtful contribution of many staff members and the energetic interest of the children from the following institutions:

HeadsUp! Development Centers and schools of the Early Learning Institute in Palo Alto, San Jose, and Pleasanton, California

The Kahakai Elementary School, Kailua-Kona, Hawaii

My experiences continue to confirm my overwhelming love for children and a great respect for their creatively playful minds as they explore the world we live in.

UNIT 1: COUNTING

INTRODUCTION

Counting goes hand-in-hand with sequencing, which children do naturally. When a child lines up blocks in a row, this is sequencing. Counting is giving number names to the objects the child has lined up. Counting and sequencing underlie higher order math skills.

Parents and caregivers are justifiably proud of their children who at an early age can recite the names of numbers ("I can count to ten!"). Although young children often correctly sequence numbers ("One, two, three . . . "), many will miscount real objects. While they can recite the names of the numbers in order, children may lack a sense of number in the abstract. They need more practice relating the number names to real world objects. As they practice this, their ability to count will grow.

The games and activities in this section invite children to extend their ability to sequence items and to count them. Since most children love to play at putting items in a row, sequencing activities provide a basis for counting and the acquisition of numbers in the abstract.

PREREQUISITE SKILLS AND CONCEPTS

Children should be able to:

1. Count out loud from one to ten and point to ten objects while giving each object a number.
2. Recognize and write numerals 0–9.
3. Put several objects (at least five) in sequence according to their numbers.
4. Know the ordinal number names "first," "second", and "third" while pointing to each item in a row of three.
5. Separate items into groups (sets) of one through ten.
6. Compare the numbers of items in separate groups.
7. Combine the items in two groups each containing at least five items, and count the combined items.

HAND-PAT COUNTING

COUNTING

> ### GOALS:
>
> - Count to 10
> - Distinguish between odd and even numbers (Extension C)
> - Begin to understand counting by 2s (Extension C)
>
> Meets NCTM Standards 2, 6, and 13
>
> ### MATERIALS:
>
> None needed

OVERVIEW

Players count to ten as they pat their hands on a table, on their legs, or on the floor. The counting can be slow or fast, out loud or silent. The leader checks during silent counting to make sure players are still counting correctly. Players can also count only even numbers while patting only one hand. This helps prepare them to count by twos, and helps them distinguish between even and odd numbers.

HOW TO PLAY THE GAME

1. Players sit in a circle.
2. The leader slowly pats one hand at a time on a table, against her leg, or the floor.
3. As she pats, she **counts** out loud.
4. The right hand is odd numbers and the left is even numbers, so the leader counts "One" (patting her right hand), "Two" (patting her left hand), and so on, up to ten.
5. Starting from one again, the players join in, patting their right hand as they count, "One," patting their left hand against the floor as they count, "Two," and so on, up to ten.

EXTENSIONS

A. As players grow used to the game, the rhythm can be speeded up.

B. Players can count silently instead of out loud. The leader stops the game in the middle of a round and asks players at what number the game stopped. This checks that players are still counting correctly.

C. The leader pats only the left hand. She counts, "One" with no pat, "Two," patting her left hand against the floor, "Three" with no pat, "Four," patting her left hand against the floor. Players join in from "One." This extension helps players distinguish **odd and even numbers,** and gives them practice in **counting by 2s.**

LEADER'S NOTES

THE WIZARD

COUNTING

GOAL:	**MATERIALS:**
• Count to 12	• 12 small blocks, large beads, etc, per player • A paper lunch bag

Meets NCTM Standards 2, 3, 5, and 6

OVERVIEW

Players reach into a bag and, without looking, count how many items they can hold in one hand. They then take the items out of the bag and count them again. This develops tactile and visual counting skills. If the players count correctly, they may keep the items, but if the count is incorrect, the items must go back into the bag. This reinforces the need for accurate counting.

HOW TO PLAY THE GAME

1. The players sit in a circle.
2. The leader puts all the blocks or beads in the paper bag.
3. The first player, Matthew, reaches into the bag with one hand only.
4. Without looking in the bag, he **counts** out loud how many blocks or beads he can hold in his hand at one time.
5. Still holding the items he just counted, Matthew takes his hand out of the bag.
6. He puts the items in front of him and counts them again out loud.
7. If the counts are accurate, Matthew can keep all the items.
8. If the two counts are different, the items must go back into the bag.
9. Players should count their items after each turn to see how many they can accumulate.

LEADER'S NOTES

SIMON SAYS "COUNT!"

COUNTING

GOALS:

- Count to 10

MATERIALS:

- None needed

Meets NCTM Standards 2, 4, and 6.

OVERVIEW

This game reinforces counting skills through movement. The leader gives instructions to perform an action a certain number of times. Players must count how many times they perform the action. Since this game is "Simon Says," only the instructions prefaced by "Simon says . . . " should be followed. Players may take turns being the leader.

Children should not be hurried in their moves. More importantly, no one should be singled out for failing to do what Simon says.

Occasionally, a player will make a wrong move. To forestall any embarrassment, invite another adult to join in and purposely make a few mistakes!

HOW TO PLAY THE GAME

1. Players stand in a circle.
2. The leader gives instructions for players to follow a specific number of times.
3. Players should only follow the instructions when the leader begins them with "Simon says . . . ."
4. If the leader does not say "Simon says . . ." before an instruction, players should not move.

Take five steps forward.

5. Instructions should be to make a certain number of movements, such as jumping, clapping, blinking, and taking steps.

6. Some instructions may be to:

- jump up and down 2 times,
- hold up 4 fingers,
- pat your knee 3 times,
- clap your hands 6 times,
- take 5 steps forward,
- take 1 step back.

7. As players perform the actions, they may **count** out loud the number of times they are doing them.

8. As the game continues, different players may take the role of the leader and give instructions to follow.

LEADER'S NOTES

"MAGIC 10" NECKLACES

COUNTING, ONE-TO-ONE CORRESPONDENCE

GOALS:

- Count to 10
- Develop sense of one-to-one correspondence

Meets NCTM Standards 2, 4, and 6.

MATERIALS:

- 10 beads to string for each player
- Yarn or string for each player

" . . . seven, eight,

OVERVIEW

By counting beads and string as they make necklaces, players use manipulatives to develop counting skills to ten. Counting the beads also helps players develop a sense of one-to-one correspondence.

HOW TO PLAY THE GAME

1. The leader puts the pieces of yarn and a pile of beads on a table.

2. The leader explains that the players will be making necklaces, and asks them to **count** the pieces of yarn, making sure there is one piece for each player.

3. Players count the pieces of yarn and each other. Luis, for example, counts 8 pieces of yarn and 8 players, including himself. This helps develop a sense of **one-to-one correspondence.**

4. The leader or a player passes out a piece of yarn to each player.

5. The leader says, "Next, we each need 10 beads. Everyone, please count out your own beads." Luis counts out 10 beads for himself from the pile on the table.

6. Players string the beads, making necklaces.

7. Players then recount the number of beads in their necklaces and in each others. Again, this helps with one-to-one correspondence.

LEADER'S NOTES

ALL ABOARD!

COUNTING, ONE-TO-ONE CORRESPONDENCE

GOALS:

- Count to 10
- Develop sense of one-to-one correspondence
- Count to 24 (Extension A)

Meets NCTM Standards 2, 4, and 6.

MATERIALS:

- 1 block to carry per player
- 2 blocks per player for Extension A

OVERVIEW

Players pretend to be cars on a freight train. Each player carries one block as freight. They unload their blocks on a table so the total can be counted and compared with the number of players. Seeing that each person carries one block and that the number of blocks on the table is the same as the number of players helps to develop a sense of one-to-one correspondence.

HOW TO PLAY THE GAME

1. Each player holds 1 block.
2. Players line up to form a freight train. They have one hand on the shoulder of the player in front of them, so all the cars of the train are connected.
3. The "train" **counts** its cars by players calling out their numbers. The first "car" says "One!," the second "car" says "Two!" and so on.
4. The train moves slowly around the room, making the appropriate "choo choo" noises.
5. When the train reaches the table, it stops for each player. Players unload their freight by putting their blocks on the table, one at a time.

6. When all the blocks are on the table, players count the blocks and count each other.

7. The leader asks, "Are there the same number of blocks as there are players?" This helps reinforce **one-to-one correspondence.**

EXTENSION

A. Each player has 2 blocks instead of one. At the end of the train's voyage, players count the blocks and each other.

LEADER'S NOTES

COUNT OFF!

COUNTING, SEQUENCING

GOALS:

- Count to 10
- Recognize written numbers to 10
- Sequence numbers to 10

MATERIALS:

- Number Cards numbered 1, 2, 3 . . . (one for each player) (pp. 76–85)

Meets NCTM Standards 2, 4, and 6

There are Number Cards on blackline masters for this game. They can be found on pages 76–85.

OVERVIEW

Players line up and count off. As the leader calls out their number, they move to the correct number card in a parallel line to the players. This helps players with sequencing, and with recognizing written numbers. In Extension A, players change numbers as their places in line change. They must recount after each shift, which reinforces sequencing.

HOW TO PLAY THE GAME

1. Players line up and count off. **Counting** off may be done several times; each player must be sure of her or his number.

2. Opposite the line of players is a line of number cards on the floor, one for each player, in the same order as the players.

3. The leader calls out a number, such as "6." Alondra is sixth in line, so she moves to stand next to the card that has "6" written on it. This helps players **recognize written numbers.**

4. The game continues until all players are standing in a line next to the number cards.

EXTENSION

A. This game starts from the new line of players next to the number cards. The leader calls out a number, such as "6." Alondra is number 6, so she moves to the head of the line. She has now become number one, and the players with numbers lower than 6 must move down one space. All players count off with their new numbers. This helps players with **sequencing.**

LEADER'S NOTES

WHAT'S MY NUMBER?

COUNTING, SEQUENCING

GOALS:

- Count to 10
- Sequencing
- Introduce ordinal numbers (Extension B)

Meets NCTM Standards 2, 4, and 6.

MATERIALS:

- Number Cards numbered 1, 2, 3 . . . (one for each player) (pp. 76–85)

There are Number Cards on blackline masters for this game. They can be found on pages 76–85.

OVERVIEW

This is a more advanced version of Count Off! (pages 12–13). Players line up in order, holding number cards. They count off. As the leader calls out numbers, the players holding those number cards walk to the table, put their cards on it, and return to their places in line. This helps develop sequencing skills. When all players have put their cards on the table, they pick up new number cards for themselves and line up in order.

This involves more sequencing, as well as counting. The game then proceeds as above. In Extension B, the leader calls out ordinal numbers, "first," "second," and so on, instead of cardinal numbers such as "one" and "two."

HOW TO PLAY THE GAME

1. Each player holds a number card.

2. Players line up in numerical order and **count** off.

3. The leader calls out a number, such as "four."

4. The player who is number four, Ashley, walks to the table, puts her card on it, and returns to her place in line. This helps develop **sequencing** skills.

5. The leader continues to call out numbers one at a time until all players have put their cards on the table and returned to their places in line.

6. The players then go to the table and pick out new numbers for themselves.

7. They form a new line, counting off with their new numbers. Ashley has chosen 7.

8. The leader calls out numbers again, as in Step 3. When seven is called, Ashley walks to the table, puts her number card on it, and returns to her place in line, again reinforcing sequencing skills.

EXTENSIONS

A. After several rounds, the leader calls out numbers in a different manner. Instead of calling "4," the leader says, "The number between 3 and 5." Ashley, number 4, counts to herself, realizes this number is her, and walks to the table to leave her card.

B. Instead of using cardinal numbers (1, 2, 3, etc.), the leader calls out **ordinal** numbers (first, second, third, and so on). This helps students learn ordinal numbers.

CUPS AND CUBES

COUNTING, COMPARING SETS

<table>
<tr><td>

GOAL:

- Count to 10
- Count to 20 or higher (Extension A)
- Reinforce sense of number

Meets NCTM Standards 2, 4, and 6.

</td><td>

MATERIALS:

- 12 to 20 small cubes for each player
- 1 cup per player, large enough to hold 20 cubes

</td></tr>
</table>

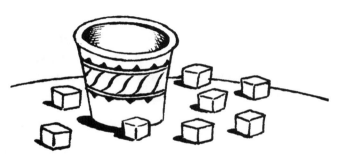

OVERVIEW

Players are given a certain number of cubes to keep in their cups. They count their own cubes and each others', seeing that each player has the same number. The leader then passes out more cubes to each player. Players then count their cubes again. This repeated counting reinforces players' sense of number and how the names of numbers relate to real objects.

HOW TO PLAY THE GAME

1. The leader gives each player a cup and 6 to 8 cubes.

2. Each player **counts** her cubes and puts them in her cup. Sarah receives 8 cubes, counts them, and puts them in her cup.

3. The leader asks each player to tell how many cubes she has. Sarah empties her cup and counts her cubes again.

4. To confirm that each player has the same number of cubes, players count their neighbors' cubes. This repeated counting reinforces players' **sense of number.**

5. The leader passes out one or two more cubes per player and asks each player to tell how many cubes she now has. Sarah counts her cubes; her total is now ten.

EXTENSION

A. Players can work in pairs, combining (hence doubling) the numbers of cubes they have. Sarah and Luis work together; they each had 10 cubes, so they count their combined cubes and discover that they now have 20. The number of cubes may be increased depending upon the counting experience of the players.

LEADER'S NOTES

I'VE GOT YOUR NUMBER!

COUNTING, SEQUENCING

GOALS:

- Count to 15
- Develop sequencing

Meets NCTM Standards 2, 4, and 6.

MATERIALS:

- Number Cards numbered 1, 2, 3 . . . (one for each player) (pp. 76–85)

Note: This game is best played outside, or in a large open space inside, as it needs quite a bit of room.

There are Number Cards on blackline masters for this game. They can be found on pages 76–85.

OVERVIEW

Players stand in a circle, holding number cards, and count off. With the players not looking, the leader taps one player on the shoulder. That player moves to the center of the circle and hides his number card. The other players use their counting and sequencing skills to guess the number of the player in the center. The player with the correct answer becomes leader for the next round.

HOW TO PLAY THE GAME

1. Each player takes a Number Card.

2. Players form a circle, according to the numbers on their cards (the numbers should be sequential).

3. Each player holds his cards so the other players can see it. The players then **count** off.

4. All players turn around so they face outward and close their eyes.

5. The leader taps one player, such as number 5, on the shoulder. That player moves to stand in the middle of the circle, hiding the number in his hand.

6. The leader then asks the other players to open their eyes and face inward again, still holding up their cards.

7. Players then use their counting and **sequencing** skills to say what number the person in the middle is. Mike, for example, sees cards 4 and 6 in the circle, but not 5. He counts to himself, "four, five, six" and realizes that player 5 is the one in the middle of the circle.

8. Mike is correct, so he becomes the leader for the next round of the game.

9. The activity can be repeated with two players being chosen to stand in the middle at the same time.

LEADER'S NOTES

TOWERS OF POWER

COUNTING, COMPARING

GOALS:

- Count to 16
- Make comparisons

MATERIALS:

- Stackable blocks, such as Unifix® cubes, up to 16 for each player

Meets NCTM Standards 2, 4, 6, and 10.

For another version of this game, involving more specific measurement, see "Taller Towers" in this section, page 28. For a more advanced version of this game, see "Twin Towers" in the Division section, page 72.

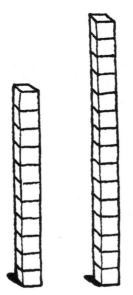

OVERVIEW

Players are given blocks to build towers with. After completing the tower, players count how many blocks tall it is and compare the height of different towers. At each new round, the leader gives out more blocks and players rebuild their towers. Players count and compare every time they build new towers. Frequent checking to see how the towers have grown underscores the importance of using counting to keep track of height and change.

HOW TO PLAY THE GAME

1. The leader gives the same number of blocks to each player (6 is a good number to start with).

2. Players are asked to build a tower with the blocks and then **count** how many blocks tall it is.

3. After building their tower and counting its blocks, players **compare** the height of each others' towers.

4. The leader gives each player 2 more blocks when they have finished building, counting, and comparing. Since players will build at different rates, this results in towers of different heights, which makes comparisons more interesting.

5. At each new height, players count the blocks to see how tall their tower has grown. They can compare heights by counting each others' blocks, and by moving their towers next to their neighbors'.

6. Useful counting and comparison questions are:

   - Whose tower is taller?
   - How many blocks do you need to make your tower as tall as Ashley's?
   - Is your tower as tall as hers?
   - Which is tallest?
   - Are any other towers the same height?

LEADER'S NOTES

MAKING TRACKS

COUNTING, ADDING

GOALS:	MATERIALS:
• Count to 30 • Introduce the basis of addition	• 10 bear tracks to put on the floor (p. 86). • Up to 30 small blocks or beads per player • 1 die (Extension A)

Meets NCTM Standards 2, 4, and 6.

OVERVIEW

Players count steps in sequence to reach ten from a designated starting point on a line. This is the simplest introduction to adding, "counting on." When players count correctly, they receive that number of blocks or beads to keep, which they recount after each turn.

HOW TO PLAY THE GAME

1. The leader sets out on the floor a row of ten unlabeled markers, placed about one child's step away from each other.

2. The leader then shows players which marker is number 1. Since the markers are not numbered, it is important for all players to **count** off the markers correctly from 1 to 10.

3. The leader calls out a number from one to eight, such as 6. The first player, Luis, counts the markers and goes to the sixth marker.

4. The player then counts how many markers there are between the one he is standing on and marker 10. Luis walks from marker 6 to marker 10 and counts 4 steps (markers). This, "counting on," introduces players to **adding,** since they are seeing that six plus four more is ten (6 + 4 = 10).

5. Luis has counted 4 correctly, so he receives 4 blocks or beads to keep.

6. If the count is incorrect, the player does not receive any blocks or beads.

7. After each round, players should recount their beads to see how many they now have.

EXTENSIONS

A. Each player rolls a single die to find the marker he or she should go to. Luis rolls a three, so he goes to the third marker and counts the number of markers between 3 and 10.

LEADER'S NOTES

BUILDING WALLS

COUNTING, ADDING

GOALS:

- Count height and width
- Introduce addition
- Introduce dimensions

Meets NCTM Standards 2, 4, 6, 9, and 10.

MATERIALS:

- Stacking blocks

Note: For a more advanced version of this game, see "Master Builder" in the Multiplication section, page 64.

OVERVIEW

Players, hearing a story about a farmer, a vegetable garden, and a pesky rabbit, build walls to keep the rabbit out of the garden. They count the width and height of the wall, as well as the total number of blocks. Since the rabbit keeps sneaking into the garden, the wall must be made wider or higher at each round. Each new wall is counted for height, width, and total number of blocks. This recounting introduces students to addition, as well as giving them experience with basic dimensions that underlie geometry.

HOW TO PLAY THE GAME

1. The leader tells a story about Farmer Brown, who has a vegetable garden. Next door lives a rabbit who eats the farmer's lettuce and other vegetables. The farmer decides to build a wall to keep the rabbit out of the garden. The wall will be 3 blocks wide and 2 blocks high.

2. The leader builds this wall, **counting** the blocks out loud as she builds. The leader counts the wall's width (3), height (2), and total number of blocks (6).

3. Each player receives 6 blocks and builds a wall with the same measurements.

4. Players count their wall's width, height, and total number of blocks.

5. Farmer Brown's story continues. The rabbit got into the garden anyway! The wall was not wide enough.

6. The leader adds 2 blocks to her wall's width, and recounts. The wall is now 4 blocks wide and 2 blocks high, and has 8 blocks total.

7. Players receive 2 more blocks each to build a wider wall. They should also recount their wall's height, width, and total number of blocks. This recount helps players see the underlying process of **addition.**

8. As the game continues, players may help Farmer Brown decide how wide and how tall each new wall should be.

LEADER'S NOTES

STEP BY STEP

COUNTING

GOALS:

- Count horizontally and vertically on a floor grid
- Find coordinates on a floor grid

Meets NCTM Standards 2, 4, 6, and 9.

MATERIALS:

- Floor grid made of string, masking tape, or chalk
- Number Cards (pp. 76–85)
- Letter Cards (p. 87–96)

A model of the floor grid appears on the opposite page. As students become more familiar with this game, the grid size can be increased to 15 x 15 or larger. Number Cards can be found on pages 76–85. Letter Cards can be found on pages 87–96.

OVERVIEW

Using a floor grid, players count the steps between two coordinates. In Extension A, the coordinates are on different axes and the number of steps will vary depending on the path taken. In Extension B, two players start at different coordinates and walk simultaneously, seeing if their paths cross.

HOW TO PLAY THE GAME

1. Use a floor grid with 10 rows and 10 columns as shown in the diagram on page 27. The rows should be labeled on the left A–J and the columns should be numbered across the top 1–10.

2. The leader shows players how to find specific coordinates, such as A2 and B3.

3. Give players lots of practice with this until they are all able to follow any row across and any column down the grid to find a specific **coordinate.**

4. Once players are comfortable, the leader gives a player a specific coordinate to stand on, such as A2. Matthew finds and stands on A2.

5. The leader asks how many squares there are between A2 and A6. Matthew walks from A2 to A6 and **counts** 4 squares.

6. Now the leader asks how many squares there are between A6 and A2. Matthew walks from A6 to A2 and counts 4 squares.

EXTENSIONS

A. Players are challenged to move across columns and rows. Matthew stands on A6, for example, and counts the squares until he reaches F6. Players may move in any direction they choose: vertically, horizontally, or diagonally. The number of squares between coordinates will vary depending on the direction taken.

B. Two players stand on different coordinates and walk at the same time, seeing if their paths will cross. For example, Matthew is on F2 and Alondra is on C7. Matthew walks to reach F10, and Alondra walks to J7 Their paths will meet at F7. However, if Matthew walks from F2 to J2 and Alondra walks from C7 to C10, their paths will not cross.

	1	2	3	4	5	6	7	8	9	10
A										
B										
C										
D										
E										
F										
G										
H										
I										
J										

TALLER TOWERS

COUNTING, MEASURING

GOALS:

- Count higher than 20
- Build to precise measurements

MATERIALS:

- Base ten number blocks OR
- Connecting Cubes (Extension B)

Meets NCTM Standards 2, 4, 6, 9, and 10

OVERVIEW

Players are given specific kinds and amounts of base ten number blocks to build towers with. Players keep an accurate count of how high their towers are, to meet precise measurements in height. The excitement of building perilously tall towers motivates players to continue, and to count again and again.

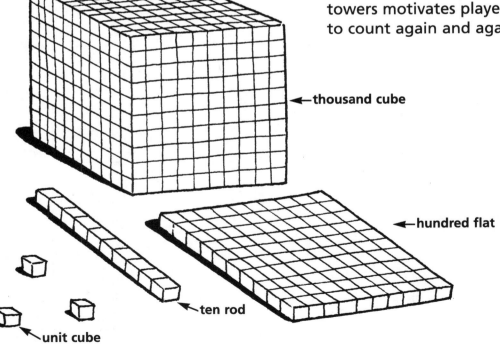

thousand cube

hundred flat

ten rod

unit cube

HOW TO PLAY THE GAME

1. The leader asks each player to become a builder.

2. Each player is given a combination of base ten number blocks. Players are asked to build each of the towers listed in Step 4.

3. **Measurements** in height are as follows:
   - 1 unit block = 1 foot high

4. Each player is supplied only the materials listed, but they do not have to use all the blocks to build their tower. Building specifications are as follows:
   - **Tower 1:** Exactly 25 feet tall. Player is given 16 unit blocks, 4 ten rods, and 5 hundred flats.
   - **Tower 2:** Exactly 39 feet tall. Player is given 10 unit blocks, 4 ten rods, 4 hundred flats, and 1 thousand cube.
   - **Tower 3:** Exactly 43 feet tall. Player is given 12 unit blocks, 6 ten rods, 4 hundred flats, and 1 thousand cube.
   - **Tower 4:** Exactly 49 feet tall. Player is given 8 unit blocks, 8 ten rods, 8 hundred flats, and 1 thousand cube.

5. Players may work in teams of two or three if they wish.

6. As they work, players must constantly **count** the height of their buildings to make sure they meet precise measurements.

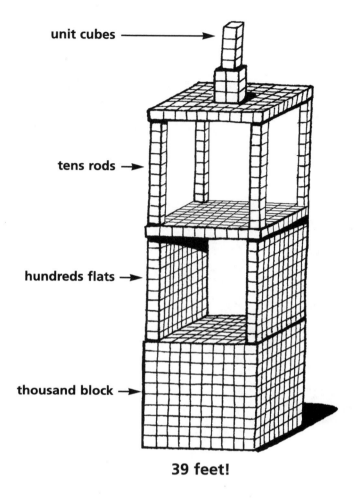

unit cubes →

tens rods →

hundreds flats →

thousand block →

39 feet!

EXTENSION

A. The leader may challenge players to build one of the above towers using all the blocks listed for that tower.

B. If base ten blocks are not available, try this using connecting cubes (Unifix®, Omnifix®, etc.). Each player uses cubes to build towers in a row, beginning with a tower (Tower A) that is 1 cube high. Next to it, the player builds another tower (Tower B) this is twice as tall as Tower A. Next to Tower B, the player builds Tower C—twice as tall as Tower B. Then the player builds Tower D twice as tall as Tower C, and so on.

UNIT 2: ADDITION AND SUBTRACTION

INTRODUCTION

Young children who are able to count to ten or higher usually have little difficulty learning to add, if the numbers they add are low (one to five), since the counting words "one, two, three, four, five" match the fingers on their hand. By touching their fingers they actively engage in counting, the basis for adding. Higher numbers can be more difficult to add, however, and some children may have trouble learning to add even lower numbers.

There are three main techniques children commonly use to add quantities or objects: sequential counting; combining objects into groups or sets; splitting up groups of items into smaller groups ("re-grouping") and then combining these smaller groups. The games in this section use each of these techniques, so all children can succeed.

Subtraction is more challenging than adding. If adding is putting on, subtracting is taking some away. Virtually all children can comprehend the process of going in the opposite direction from adding.

Actually, for children to reverse the adding process successfully requires more than just taking away. They must continually count the quantities involved during the operation. These games emphasize counting at the same time as they reinforce addition and subtraction skills, all within enjoyable contexts. Children are engaged in each game and are encouraged to learn from their experience, so that addition and subtraction become a natural outgrowth of their counting skill.

PREREQUISITE SKILLS AND CONCEPTS

Children should be able to:

1. Recognize, say, and write the numerals one through ten.

2. Count to 20 and point to corresponding items in a group.

3. Sequence ten items, and count in any order the items in a group of ten.

4. Say the first ten ordinal numbers while pointing to ten items in sequence.

5. Separate ten items into two or more groups and then count the number of groups as well as the items within each group.

6. Combine in either order two groups of fewer than ten items and count the total number of items in the combined group.

ADD TAG

ADDING, COUNTING

GOAL:

- Add single-digit numbers

MATERIALS:

- Number Cards numbered 1, 2, 3 . . . (one for each player) (pp. 76–85)

Meets NCTM Standards 2, 4, 6 and 8.

Four plus three is seven.

There are Number Cards on blackline masters for this game. They can be found on pages 76–85.

OVERVIEW

Instead of forming a number line, players stand in a number circle, holding sequentially numbered cards and count off. The player who is "It" walks around the outside of the circle until told by the leader to stop. "It" adds out loud the number on his or her Number Card plus the number on the card of the nearest player. If the sum is not correct, the "It" player remains "It" for the next round. If the sum is correct, the player whose number was added becomes "It."

HOW TO PLAY THE GAME

1. Players form a circle, facing inward and standing about an arm's length apart from each other. The leader stands in the middle of the circle.

2. Each player is given a sequentially numbered card to hold.

3. Players **count** off in the same order as the cards.

4. The leader points to a player, Ashley, who becomes "It."

5. Ashley, "It," walks clockwise around the outside of the circle until the leader calls "Stop."

6. Ashley goes to the player closest to her, Mike, who shows Ashley his Number Card.

7. Ashley **adds** Mike's number with the number on her own card and says the sum out loud.

8. If Ashley is correct, she goes back to her place in the circle and Mike becomes "It" for the next round.

9. If Ashley's sum is not correct, she remains "It" for the next round.

LEADER'S NOTES

NUMBER NAMES

ADDING, COUNTING

GOALS:

- Add 1 to a number
- Add 2 to a number (Extension A)

MATERIALS:

None needed.

Meets NCTM Standards 2, 4, 6 and 8.

OVERVIEW

Players stand in a circle and introduce themselves to each other, using numbers as their names. The leader is "One" and each player must add one to the number name of the player before him. The player next to the leader adds one plus one to get "Two" for his name; the following player must add two plus one for the name of "Three." After all players have introduced themselves, the leader calls on players to perform various actions a certain number of times.

My name is One Plus One, which is Two

HOW TO PLAY THE GAME

1. Players and the leader form a circle, facing inward.

2. The leader begins by turning to the player on her left, Luis and saying, "Hello, my name is One. What's your name?"

3. Luis must **add** one to the previous number name to give his number name.

4. Luis adds one plus one and answers, "My name is One plus One, which is Two."

5. He then turns to the player on his left, Sarah and says, "Hello, my name is Two. What's your name?"

6. Sarah adds one to Luis' number name to give her number name. She says, "My name is Two plus One, which is Three."

7. When each player has added and given his or her number name, the leader calls on one player and asks him to perform an action. For example, "Two, clap your hands three times." Luis claps his hands three times.

8. Luis has completed the action successfully, so it is now his turn to call on someone else to perform an action.

EXTENSION

A. The players add by twos instead of ones. The leader says, "Hello, my name is Two. What's your name?" Luis adds 2 plus 2 and says, "My name is Two plus Two, which is Four."

LEADER'S NOTES

SECRET AGENTS

ADDING

GOALS:

- Add numbers to 1 through 26
- Introduce the use of symbols

Meets NCTM Standards 1, 2, 4, 6, 7, 8 and 13.

MATERIALS:

- Pencils for each student
- Paper for each student

Note: As an optional activity, copy one Secret Agent Identification card for each player. Have each player cut out the card and write in her secret code in the blanks provided.

For a similar game involving subtraction, see "007," page 56.

OVERVIEW

Players create codes from numbers representing letters of the alphabet. In the base code, a = 1, b = 2 and so on; players add one to the base code to create a secret code. As players gain experience, they can add any number to the base code for their own private code. As well as providing adding practice, this game introduces players to the concept of symbols: a specific sign used in place of another sign.

HOW TO PLAY THE GAME

1. The leader displays the base code (See below.) for the players. The code is the alphabet with a number next to each letter, **symbolizing** that letter. In this code, a = 1, b = 2, c = 3 and so on.

2. Players practice writing with this code. "Sarah," for example, would be "19 1 18 1 8."

3. Once players are comfortable using this code, the leader explains that to create a real secret code, they can add a number to the base code.

4. Players add one to the base code, so that a = 2, b = 3, c = 4, etc. "Sarah" now is "20 2 19 2 9."

5. Players may **add** one or any other number they are comfortable with to create their own secret code.

ACTIVE MATH
SECRET AGENT IDENTIFICATION CARD

— — — — — — — — — —

— — — — — — — — — —

Warning: only certified **ACTIVE MATH SECRET AGENTS** can read this secret code name!

A = 1	**H** = 8	**O** = 15	**V** = 22
B = 2	**I** = 9	**P** = 16	**W** = 23
C = 3	**J** = 10	**Q** = 17	**X** = 24
D = 4	**K** = 11	**R** = 18	**Y** = 25
E = 5	**L** = 12	**S** = 19	**Z** = 26
F = 6	**M** = 13	**T** = 20	
G = 7	**N** = 14	**U** = 21	

GO FETCH!

ADDING

GOALS:

- Repeated addition
- Introduce basis for multiplication

MATERIALS:

- Markers to use as "houses" (1 for each "owner")
- Markers to use as "sticks" (up to 5 for each "dog")

Meets NCTM Standards 2, 3, 4, 6, 7, 8 and 13.

OVERVIEW

Players form pairs of "dogs" and "owners." Each owner has a house and each dog is given a stick at each round. Players repeatedly add the numbers of sticks, dogs, owners and houses. This repeated addition lays the groundwork for the process of multiplication.

HOW TO PLAY THE GAME

1. Players form pairs. One player will be the "owner" and the other player will be the "dog."

2. The leader begins a story. On a quiet street next to a large field live some people. (The number of people in the story should be the same as the number of pairs of players, such as 4.) Each of these people has a dog and a house.

3. The leader passes out a "house" marker to each owner.

4. Players now **add** together the number houses on the street to find how many houses there are (4, in this example).

5. They then add the number of dogs to find how many dogs there are (4).

6. Next they add the number of owners to find how many owners there are (4).

7. The leader says, "Add together the number of houses, plus the number of dogs, plus the number of people. What is the total?" (12)

8. This **repeated addition** gives players a basis for multiplication.

9. The leader continues with the story. One day, all the owners take their dogs out to play in the large field. Each dog finds a stick.

10. The leader passes out a "stick" marker to each "dog."

11. Players add the number of sticks to find how many sticks there are (4).

12. They then add the number of dogs plus the number of sticks to find that total (8).

13. Finally, they add together the number of dogs, sticks and owners (12).

14. This repeated addition is helpful as an introductory basis for multiplication.

15. Players may now switch roles or remain as "owner" and "dog."

16. The story continues; with each visit to the park, the dogs find 1 more stick to add to their collection.

EXTENSION

A. While playing in the field, each dog finds 2, 3, or 4 sticks at a time. This gives players practice adding with higher numbers.

CARS AND DRIVERS

ADDING, ESTIMATING

GOALS:

- Add to 55
- Begin to estimate

Meets NCTM Standards 2, 4, 5, 6 and 8.

MATERIALS:

- Sets of cards numbered 1–10 (one set for each team)

Note A: Players may enjoy helping to sort the cards into piles by number.

Note B: This game is best played in a gym or large open area as it requires a great deal of activity.

OVERVIEW

Players pair up as "car" and "driver" to pick up as many number cards as they can. The cards are piled together according to number. Players may take only one card from each pile. The game is timed at two minutes. Players must pick up cards, return to the starting point and add up their totals within the time limit. The lowest-numbered cards are closest and the highest-numbered cards are farthest away.

By going farther, players can pick up higher-numbered cards, but they use up more time doing so. They must estimate the best way to use their time. This game fosters cooperation between players as they collect cards and add their numbers together. In the next round, players switch roles and try to improve their scores.

HOW TO PLAY THE GAME

1. Sort the number cards so all the 1s are in one pile, all the 2s are in another pile and so on.

2. Mark a starting point and show players where it is.

3. The leader places the piles of cards at various distances from the starting point. The lower-numbered cards should be closer to the starting point and the higher-numbered cards should be farther away.

4. Players pair up. One is the "car" and the other is the "driver."

5. The driver stands behind the car, hands on the car's shoulders. The driver will steer and stop the car.

6. All pairs line up behind the starting point.

7. The leader explains to the players that they will have two minutes to collect their cards and **add** them up.

8. The leader continues to explain that "speeding" (running) is not allowed. Speeders will receive a "speeding ticket," of 5 points, which will be subtracted from their total.

9. When the leader says "Start," drivers steer their cars to a pile.

10. The car picks up one card from that pile.

11. The driver then steers the car to another pile.

12. The leader tells the players when one minute is up, and then says "Stop," when two minutes are up.

13. Players must collect as many cards as they can, return to the starting point and add up the total on their cards within the two-minute time limit.

14. Since the higher-numbered cards are farther away, players must estimate the best way to use their limited time. They will get more points with the higher cards, but will have less time to pick up cards.

15. If players do not add up their cards correctly, they do not receive any points.

16. There is one more round; cars and drivers switch roles and try to improve their scores.

BLOCK PARTY

ADDING, COUNTING, GROUPING

GOALS:

- Add different quantities to reach the same sum
- Count up to 10
- Start to use mathematical symbols and equations

Meets NCTM Standards 1, 2, 3, 4, 6, 7, 8 and 13.

MATERIALS:

- 1 block per player (or at least 6 blocks total)
- Pencil and paper for the leader

Two plus four is six!

OVERVIEW

Players have a certain number of blocks. They divide the blocks into different groups, counting them and seeing how many combinations of blocks still add up to the original number. The leader writes each new combination down as an equation and explains it to the players. This serves as a model for using mathematical symbols and illustrates the adding process.

HOW TO PLAY THE GAME

1. The leader shows the players a group of blocks.

2. There should be at least 1 block for each player; if there are fewer than 6 players, use a minimum of 6 blocks.

3. The leader asks, "How many blocks do I have?" Players **count** the blocks and answer. Mike, for example, counts and answers, "Six."

4. The leader then separates 2 blocks from the other 4 and asks, "How many blocks are there in this group?" Mike counts and replies, "Two."

5. The leader asks, "How many blocks are there in the other group?" Mike counts again and replies, "Four."

6. The last question is, "Are there still six blocks total?" Mike **adds** the blocks together and says, "Yes."

7. The players are now given the blocks and are asked how many different combinations or groups of blocks they can come up with that still add up to six. Possibilities include a group of 4 and a group of 2, 2 groups of 3, 1 group of 5 and 1 block, 1 group of 6 and 1 group of 0 (assuming players are familiar with the counting number "0").

8. As players develop combinations, the leader writes them down as equations. The equation for a group of two and a group of four, for instance, is $2 + 4 = 6$.

9. The leader shows players the equations for each new combination, explaining them. (The 2 blocks in this group plus the 4 blocks in that group add together to equal 6.)

THE ARCHER

ADDING, ESTIMATING, GROUPING

GOALS:

- Add 2 or more numbers together to equal 10
- Estimate length
- Develop understanding of the commutative principle of addition

Meets NCTM Standards 1, 2, 3, 4, 5, 6, 7, 8, 10 and 13.

MATERIALS:

- Number line from 1–10 (p. 98)
- 2 sets of unmarked arrows (pp. 99–100) (each arrow in a set reaches one number on the number line)

Note: For a version of this game involving subtraction, see "Counting Backwards," page 54.

The blackline master on the opposite page is for keeping score. You may opt to make copies of the score sheet and distribute one to each player.

Other blackline masters for this game are the Number Line (page 98) and the Arrows (pages 99–100). Please refer to the blackline masters for instructions on how they should be used.

OVERVIEW

Players first estimate which arrow or arrows will reach a certain point on the number line. They then pick out the arrows and measure the span. Players add the lengths of the arrows as they find two or more arrows that together reach a longer length. They also discover that the order in which the arrows are placed on the number line does not affect the total length, illustrating the commutative principle of addition.

HOW TO PLAY THE GAME

1. The leader shows players the number line and the arrows and helps them see that each arrow reaches a different number on the number line.

2. Players are asked to find the arrow that reaches from 0 to 6 on the number line.

3. They **estimate** which arrow is the correct length and try different arrows until they find the correct one.

4. The leader repeats this with different numbers, until all players are comfortable with estimating the lengths of the arrows.

5. The leader then places the 6 arrow on the number line.

6. She asks players to find two arrows that, when put together, measure the same distance that the 6 arrow does.

7. Players again estimate the length of different arrows and **add** their lengths together to make sure they equal the correct number. Ashley, for instance,

adds a 1 and a 5 arrow together to measure 6.

8. The leader then asks, "If you change the order of those two arrows, what happens? Do they still add up to 6?"

9. Ashley changes the order of the arrows so they are now a 5 and a 1 arrow. She adds 5 and 1 together and finds the sum is still the same. This illustrates the commutative principle of addition (a + b = b + a, or 1 + 5 = 5 + 1).

10. The game continues with players finding arrows that, combined, add up to different numbers on the line.

11. The leader makes copies of the score sheet below and distributes one to each player. Each time a player gets a correct answer, she colors in a ring working from the outside to the center. Each ring should be a different color. Once the player gets five correct answers and colors in the final ring, she gets a bull's eye!

EXTENSIONS

A. Using both sets of arrows, players find how many different arrows it can take to add up to a certain number on the line. For example, Ashley finds that 2 + 1 + 3 adds up to six, or that 1 + 1 + 2 + 2 also adds up to six. This is a further example of the grouping and commutative principle of addition.

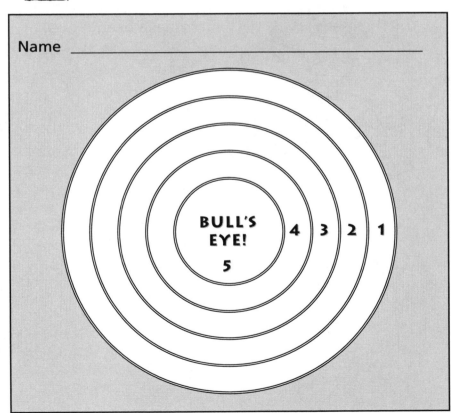

Name _____

BULL'S EYE!

5

4

3

2

1

SUPER WIZARD

ADDING, COUNTING

GOAL:

- Add to 20

Meets NCTM Standards 1, 2, 3, 6 and 8.

MATERIALS:

- 2 paper lunch bags for each pair of players
- 20 blocks (all 1 color) for each player
- 20 blocks, divided evenly between 2 colors, for each player (Extension A)

Note: For a version of this game involving subtraction, see "Abracadabra," page 60.

OVERVIEW

Players form pairs. One player moves blocks from one bag to the next; the other player must add up the blocks, without looking in either bag, to find how many have been moved.

HOW TO PLAY THE GAME

1. Players form pairs. Each pair has 2 paper bags and 2 sets of blocks.

2. The first player, Luis, **counts** out 4 blocks.

3. He puts 1 block in one bag and 3 blocks in the other bag while his partner, Alondra, watches.

4. Luis then moves 2 blocks from the second bag to the first bag as Alondra looks on.

5. Alondra must now tell Luis how many blocks are in the first bag, without looking inside.

6. She adds the 2 blocks that were moved, plus the 1 block that was there before, to equal three.

7. Luis empties the first bag so both players can see if Alondra's answer was correct.

8. Alondra has added correctly, so she keeps the three blocks.

9. If Alondra didn't add correctly, Luis would keep the blocks.

10. It is Alondra's turn next to place blocks inside the bags.

11. As the game continues, more blocks are used in each round.

EXTENSION

A. Players use blocks of two different colors mixed together in the bag. They then add how many blocks of each color and how many blocks total are in the first bag, as in Step 5 above.

LEADER'S NOTES

TAKE IT TO THE BANK

ADDING, COUNTING, PLACE VALUE

GOALS:

- Add to 19
- Count to 12
- Develop understanding of place value

Meets NCTM Standards 2, 3, 4, 6, 7, 8, and 13.

MATERIALS:

- Base ten number blocks *or* Base ten Fun Money, page 101
- 2 or 3 dice
- Recording Sheets for each player, page 102
- Pencils for each player

There are two blackline masters for this game. Fun Money (page 101) can be used if base ten blocks are unavailable. Fun Money comes in units (cents), tens (dimes), and hundreds (dollars). Students may enjoy coloring all the units one color, all the tens another color, and all the hundreds a third color. This will also make the money more easily identifiable.

Use of the Recording Sheet (page 102) is explained in How to Play the Game, steps 5, 6, 10, and 11.

Nine!

OVERVIEW

Players roll the dice and **add** up the number of dots to earn base ten blocks or Fun Money. Whenever a player earns ten of any kind of block, he or she turns them into the bank in exchange for one of the next larger block. Through this exchange process, students begin to understand how the base ten counting system works.

Players **count** their earnings after each turn, and add their new earnings to their previous total. They also record their totals after each turn, writing the amount of each kind of block on their Recording Sheets. This counting, adding, and recording helps students develop an understanding of place value.

HOW TO PLAY THE GAME

1. The leader plays the role of the banker and holds all the "money" (the blocks).

2. Each player earns blocks by rolling 2 dice and adding up the number of dots shown.

3. Players have to add the numbers on 2 dice correctly in order to earn blocks. If this is too difficult, see Extension A.

4. If the player adds correctly, she receives that amount in base ten blocks. For example, if Sarah correctly adds "9" on her turn, she receives 9 unit blocks, or the equivalent of 9 cents.

5. After each turn, players count their blocks and write the total on their Recording Sheet. The first column on the sheet is hundreds (dollars), the second column is tens (dimes), and the third column is units (pennies). Since Sarah has 9 unit blocks, she writes "9" in the third column.

6. By writing the amounts in the correct columns of the Recording Sheets, players begin to understand place value.

7. On each subsequent turn, players roll the dice and add up the sum. Sarah correctly adds "5" on her next turn.

8. Players then count the blocks they receive and add them to their previous total. Sarah counts the 5 unit blocks she receives and adds them to the 9 unit blocks she already has. She now has 14 unit blocks.

9. When a player has 10 of any block, she trades them to the bank for 1 of the next higher blocks. Sarah trades in 10 of her unit blocks for 1 ten rod.

10. The player then counts her blocks and writes the new total on her Recording Sheet. Sarah writes "1" in the tens column (because she has one ten rod) and "4" in the units column (because she also has four unit blocks). Sarah's total is fourteen cents.

11. This exchange with the bank and the use of the Recording Sheet helps students understand place value.

12. The Recording Sheets also allow players to turn their blocks into the bank and stop playing at any time. The sheets will contain a record of their earnings for the next time they want to play.

EXTENSIONS

A. Use only 1 die for very young students or for students who have trouble adding 2 dice together.

B. For older children or those with more experience of real-life money, the dice can represent tens instead of units. For example, if a player rolls a "9," he receives the equivalent of 90 cents.

C. As the players gain in skill, the leader can introduce a third die. Students roll 3 dice at one time and correctly add up the numbers shown to earn blocks.

D. For a more advanced version of this game, see "You Can Bank on It!" on page 66 of the Multiplication section.

ADD IT UP!

ADDING, COUNTING

GOALS:

- Add base ten number blocks to find 2-, 3- and 4-digit numbers
- Use mathematical symbols
- Write down 2-, 3- and 4-digit numbers

Meets NCTM Standards 1, 2, 3, 4, 6, 7, 8 and 13.

MATERIALS:

- Base ten number blocks

OVERVIEW

The leader sets out base ten number blocks representing a two-digit number. Players look at the blocks and add them to find the number being represented. When the player is correct, he writes down the number. This game continues with three- and four-digit numbers being represented by base ten number blocks. In Extension A, players must add two sets of number blocks together to find their sum. In Extensions B and C, players are given written numbers and must find the correct number blocks to represent them. Matching symbols with the objects they symbolize provides the basis for other mathematical operations.

Twenty plus three is twenty-three.

HOW TO PLAY THE GAME

1. The leader puts on a table base ten number blocks representing a two digit number. If the number is 23, for instance, the leader puts out two ten rods and three unit cubes.

2. The first player, Mike, looks at the number blocks and **adds** them up.

3. If he adds them correctly, he writes down the number. This gives him experience using **mathematical symbols.**

4. If he doesn't add correctly, he doesn't write anything down.

5. The leader puts out a combination of blocks for the next player to add.

6. When all players have had a turn with two-digit numbers, the leader sets out blocks that represent a three-digit number and the game proceeds as above.

7. The next step is for the leader to set out blocks that represent four-digit numbers.

EXTENSIONS

A. The leader sets out two piles of blocks each time instead of one. Players add the two piles together and, if correct, write down the sum.

B. The leader writes down a two-, three-, or four-digit number. Players must find the base ten number blocks that represent this number and arrange them in the correct order. This gives players further experience with mathematical symbolization.

C. The leader writes down two numbers. Players must first add the two numbers together and then find the correct number blocks to represent their sum.

LEADER'S NOTES

BIRDS OF A FEATHER

SUBTRACTING, COUNTING

GOALS:

- Introduce subtraction
- Subtract from 5 and 10
- Count to 10

MATERIALS:

- 2 hands
- Finger puppets (page 97), blocks, or other objects.

Meets NCTM Standards 2, 4, 6 and 8.

There is a blackline master for the finger puppets in this game. Please refer to page 97 for the blackline master and instructions on how to create the finger puppets.

OVERVIEW

The leader cuts out the page of finger puppets and asks the children to color and then tape them together to make finger puppets. The leader then places the puppets on her fingers to represent birds sitting on a branch. She puts out one hand with five fingers for players to count and then tucks in two fingers. Players count the remaining fingers, which introduces subtraction. Players work up to all ten fingers, being introduced to subtraction through the number ten. In Variation A, players are asked to subtract the remaining fingers to see how many are missing.

HOW TO PLAY THE GAME

1. The leader spreads out 5 fingers of one hand with the finger puppets placed on them.

2. Players **count** the finger puppets on the leader's fingers.

3. The leader then says, "These are 5 birds sitting on a branch. If 2 birds fly away, how many will be left?"

4. The leader tucks 2 fingers under so only 3 are visible.

5. Players count the remaining fingers puppets to find how many birds are left (3). This introduces **subtraction.**

6. The game continues, with different amounts of birds sitting and leaving, gradually working up to all 10 fingers.

EXTENSION

A. Players close their eyes while the leader puts out her hand with 3 fingers showing. She says, "Open your eyes. There were 5 birds here before. How many have flown away?" Players **subtract** 3 from 5 to find that 2 birds have flown away. This continues with varying numbers of fingers, working up to all 10.

B. The leader sets out blocks (or beads) instead of fingers and repeats the process. Players must close their eyes while the leader removes several blocks. The players now look and count the remaining ones. The first player to tell correctly how many "birds" flew away gets to take the next turn as the leader. This game also can be played by pairs of players, who take turns being the leader.

COUNTING BACKWARDS

SUBTRACTING, GROUPING

GOALS:

- Subtract from 20
- Introduce mathematical equations

Meets NCTM Standards 1, 2, 3, 4, 5, 6, 7, 8, 10 and 13.

MATERIALS:

- Number line from 1–20 (p. 98)
- 2 sets of unmarked arrows (pp. 99–100)(each arrow in a set reaches one number on the number line)

Note: For a version of this game involving addition, see "The Archer," page 44.

There are three blackline masters for this game. A Number Line (page 98) and the Arrows (pages 99–100). Please refer to the blackline masters for instructions on how they should be used.

OVERVIEW

Players use the number line and the unmarked arrows, to subtract from a specific number, which should be determined by the leader. Players learn that in order to subtract on the number line, they place the arrow in the opposite direction from that used when adding, as in "The Archer." After players find the correct arrows to subtract with, the leader states the answer in an equation reflecting the players' solutions.

HOW TO PLAY THE GAME

1. The leader picks a starting point greater than 10 on the number line, such as 14.

2. The leader asks a player, Sarah, to find the arrow whose length is shorter than 14. Sarah finds a "6" arrow.

3. The leader then asks Sarah to put the "6" arrow on the starting point, 14, with the point of the arrow facing left on the line towards the smaller numbers.

4. The leader asks, "What number does the arrow point to?"

5. Sarah answers, "Eight."

6. The leader writes this into an **equation** and says, "So, 14 - 6 = 8." This helps to teach players **subtraction.**

7. These steps are repeated with different numbers so all players have a turn.

8. The leader repeats the equation each time. As players grow more confident with subtraction, they can take turns saying the equation.

EXTENSIONS

A. The leader starts at 14. She marks another point below that, such as 8, and asks players to find the arrow that points backwards from 14 to 8. Players find that arrow and identify its length. This equation is still 14 - 6 = 8.

B. Players find two arrows that together point backwards from 14 to 8. These could be a 1 and a 5, a 2 and a 4, or a 3 and a 3. Players find the lengths of the individual arrows and add their lengths together.

C. Players find three arrows that, laid end to tip pointing backwards, total 6. The last arrow must point to 8. These arrows can be any combination of three lengths that equal 6. The leader can challenge players to discover for themselves the different combinations of arrows. (There are three, excluding 6 and 0: 1 + 2 + 3, 2 + 2 + 2, and 4 + 1 + 1.)

007

SUBTRACTING

GOALS:

- Subtract 10 from a number
- Subtract from 36
- Introduce mathematical symbols

Meets NCTM Standards 1, 2, 4, 6, 7, 8 and 13.

MATERIALS:

- Pencil for each player
- Paper for each player

Note: For a similar game involving addition, see "Secret Agents," page 36.

OVERVIEW

Players create codes with numbers representing letters of the alphabet. In the base code, a=11, b=12 and so on; players subtract 10 from the base code to create a secret code. As players gain experience, they can subtract any number from the base code for their own private code. As well as providing subtraction practice, this gives players more experience with symbols: a specific sign used in place of another sign.

HOW TO PLAY THE GAME

1. The leader writes down the base code. The base code should be a = 11, b = 12, c = 13 and so on.

2. Players practice using this base code. "Alondra," for example, would be: "11 22 25 24 14 28 11."

3. Once players are comfortable using this base code, they can develop their own secret codes by **subtracting** a number from the base code. (To avoid the use of negative numbers, players should not subtract any numbers greater than 10.)

4. Players subtract 10 from the base code, so that a = 1, b = 2, c = 3 and so on. "Alondra" is now: "1 12 15 14 4 18 1."

5. As players become more comfortable with the game, they can create their own private codes, subtracting any number between 1 and 10 from the base code.

6. Use of the codes gives players practice working with **symbols.**

EXTENSION

A. Players start with a higher base code for more challenge. They can create their own base code as well as their secret variations on it.

SHEEP IN A STORM

SUBTRACTING, COUNTING

GOALS:

- Subtract from 12
- Subtract from 24 (Extension A) and 36 (Extension B)
- Count to 12
- Count to 24 (Extension A) and 36 (Extension B)

Meets NCTM Standards 1, 2, 3, 4, 6, 7 and 8.

MATERIALS:

- Up to 36 blocks to stack
- 12 paper sheep (See blackline master on page 104.), beads or other small markers to represent sheep

There are blackline masters on pages 103–4 for this game. Players can cut, color, and apply cotton balls to the blackline master on page 104 to represent sheep.

Model A on page 103 shows the pen in its starting shape, before the storm (see Step 1). Models B–F show various shapes of the pen after some blocks have been washed away (see Steps 3 and 9). Each model shows the number of blocks needed for the main version of the game. Extension A doubles the number of blocks and Extension B triples the number of blocks.

OVERVIEW

The leader tells a story about Farmer Fernandez, who keeps some sheep in a pen. One day, a storm comes, washing away part of the pen and allowing some of the sheep to run away.

The leader builds a pen with 12 blocks and puts the 12 sheep markers inside the pen. The leader then removes three blocks and three sheep. Players count the remaining sheep and subtract that number from 12 to find the number of sheep that have run away. They also count the remaining blocks and subtract that number from 12 to find how many blocks have been washed away by the storm.

Players then rebuild the pen and the sheep return. At each round, another storm comes, washing away varying amounts of blocks and allowing varying numbers of sheep to escape.

Blackline masters Models B–F show shapes of the pen after the storms. In Extensions A and B, Farmer Fernandez builds the wall two and three blocks high, but it still washes away.

HOW TO PLAY THE GAME

1. The leader explains that Farmer Fernandez has 12 sheep in a pen made of 12 blocks. One night there was a big storm that washed away some of the blocks of the pen and some of the sheep ran away.

2. The leader makes a pen of 12 blocks (see blackline master Model A on page 103) and puts 12 markers inside for sheep.

3. Players close their eyes while the leader takes away 3 blocks from the pen and removes 3 sheep. (See blackline master Model B, page 103, for the new pen shape.)

4. Players open their eyes and look at the pen. The leader says, "There used to be 12 sheep in the pen. How many ran away?"

5. Players **count** the remaining sheep and subtract that number (9) from 12. The answer is "3."

6. Next the leader says, "There were 12 blocks making up the walls of the pen before the storm. How many blocks were washed away by the storm?"

7. Players count the remaining blocks and subtract that number (9) from 12 to find the correct answer of 3.

8. Players then help Farmer Fernandez rebuild the pen, counting to make sure they are using the correct number of blocks, and the sheep return.

9. The game repeats, with the storm washing away different amounts of blocks each time and allowing different numbers of sheep to run away. (See blackline master Models C-F, page 103, for the different pen shapes.)

10. Players count and subtract to find the number of missing sheep and missing blocks at each round.

EXTENSIONS

A. The sheep are bigger and stronger now, so the farmer has made the walls of the pen two blocks high instead of one. The diagrams on page 103 can still be used for the pen shapes. The total number of blocks is now 24. Players now **subtract** from 24 to find the missing number of blocks.

B. The walls of the pen are now 3 blocks high. Players subtract from 36 to find how many blocks have washed away. The diagrams on page 103 can still be used for the pen shapes.

ABRACADABRA!

SUBTRACTING, COUNTING, GROUPING

GOAL:

- Subtract from 20
- Count to 20

Meets NCTM Standards 1, 2, 3, 6 and 8.

MATERIALS:

- 2 paper lunch bags for each pair of players
- 20 blocks (all one color) for each player
- 20 blocks, divided evenly between two colors, for each player (Extension A)

Note: For a version of this game involving addition, see "Super Wizard," page 46.

OVERVIEW

Players work in pairs. One player counts out blocks in a bag, and moves some of them from one bag to the next; the other player must subtract to find out how many blocks have been left in the first bag.

HOW TO PLAY THE GAME

1. Players form pairs. Each pair has 2 paper bags and a pile of 20 blocks.

2. The first player, Sarah, puts 6 blocks into the first bag.

3. Sarah then counts out a number of blocks from the first bag and puts them in the second bag while her partner, Luis, watches.

4. Luis must now tell Sarah how many blocks are left in the first bag without looking inside either bag.

5. He **subtracts** the blocks that Sarah moved from the 6 original blocks to find the answer of three. If she moved 3, the answer is 3.

6. If Luis subtracts correctly, he may keep the 3 blocks.

7. If Luis doesn't subtract correctly, Sarah keeps the three blocks.

8. The players switch roles for the next round.

9. As the game continues, the players can increase the number of blocks.

EXTENSION

A. Players use blocks of two different colors mixed together. They count how many blocks of each color there are to begin with and subtract to find how many remain of each color after Step 3 is repeated.

LEADER'S NOTES

UNIT 3: MULTIPLICATION AND DIVISION

INTRODUCTION

Multiplying and dividing demand a whole new way of thinking about numbers. The difference lies in the function of the numbers. Multiplying and dividing require that one of the numbers not be viewed as a quantity at all. Instead one of them functions as an operator. That is, one number tells what operation to perform on the other number.

Consider from a child's viewpoint the difference between the process of addition (or subtraction) and multiplication. In the process of addition, for example, a three plus a two equal five. We write that as a number sentence: 3 + 2 = 5. Each number stands for a separate, designated quantity of things. The plus sign (+) between three and two says to us: "put those two quantities together." Similarly, in subtraction the minus sign between the two numbers means: "take the second quantity away from the first," as in the number sentence 3 - 2 = 1.

When children begin learning about the processes of multiplication, they run into a sharp contrast. When three and two are multiplied (3 x 2), no longer do both numbers stand for quantities. Only one numeral stands for a quantity! The other numeral tells us how many times to "add" the quantity (or group). The times sign (x) in the process of repeated addition (which is one way of describing multiplication) means either add the group of three two times, or it means add the quantity of two three times! This difference perplexes many children at the very start of their introduction to multiplication.

In division, the reverse of multiplication, the two numerals again do not both stand for quantities. In the number sentence 8 ÷ 4 = ? it is only the first numeral that symbolizes a quantity. The sign ÷ means: "find out how many times the second quantity occurs within the first," or, "find out how many groups of 4 are in 8."

A further confusion grows for many children when they must differentiate between multiplying two numbers and dividing them. In multiplying, the operation can be done in either direction. For example two groups of four is equivalent to four groups of two. In division, however, the quantity given must be broken into a specified number of groups, which does not allow the operation to be done in either direction.

PREREQUISITE SKILLS AND CONCEPTS

Children should be able to:

1. Perform all the skills listed in the Introduction to Unit 2: Addition and Subtraction.

2. Separate 20 items into multiple groups of equal size, and then count the number of groups as well the items within all the groups.

3. Combine in any order three groups of at least ten in each and count the total number.

MASTER BUILDER

MULTIPLYING, DIVIDING, ADDING, COUNTING

GOALS:

- Count to 30
- Add to 30
- Introduction to multiplication
- Introduction to dimensions: height, width, and depth
- Introduction to division
- Experience with mathematical equations

Meets NCTM Standards 1, 2, 3, 4, 6, 7, 8, 9, 10 and 13.

MATERIALS:

- Up to 30 building blocks for each player, all one size

Note: For a simpler version of this game, see "Building Walls," page 24.

OVERVIEW

Players build walls according to specific dimensions, such as three blocks high, two blocks wide and three blocks deep. They must first count the blocks to use and, while building, double up rows of blocks to make walls the correct height. This doubling up introduces players to multiplication. As they build, players must also evenly portion out blocks from the total they have, which introduces them to division. Players must also count how many blocks they have in each row and add them together to make sure they use the correct number of blocks. In Extension A, the leader writes down the wall measurements in equation form.

HOW TO PLAY THE GAME

1. The leader gives players a certain measurement for a wall, such as 2 blocks high, 2 blocks wide, and one block deep.

2. Players, working alone, must build a wall that exactly matches these **dimensions.**

3. Ashley **counts** out 4 blocks to use for her wall.

4. All players will measure their walls as they build, so if they count out the wrong number of blocks at this step, they will catch that mistake later on.

5. Ashley divides her blocks into 2 groups, 1 for each row.

6. As she builds, she doubles the blocks up to make the wall the correct dimensions; this doubling up introduces her to **multiplication.**

7. After she builds the wall, Ashley recounts the blocks she has used to make sure the wall matches its specifications. If she counted out her blocks incorrectly in Step 3, she will find her mistake here, as she measures her wall again.

8. The leader gives her the measurements for the next wall to build, say 3 blocks high, 2 blocks wide, and 1 block deep.

9. Ashley takes apart the wall she just built and counts out the number of blocks she needs for the new wall.

10. The game continues, with the dimensions increasing in complexity at each new round.

EXTENSIONS

A. When the walls are successfully built, the leader writes down the measurements in **equation** form. For the wall in Steps 1–7 above, the equation is 2 x 2 x 1 = 4. This gives players a further introduction to multiplication and to mathematical equations.

B. The leader gives players a certain number of blocks and asks them to build walls of as many different shapes as possible, using only those blocks.

YOU CAN BANK ON IT!

MULTIPLYING, ADDING, COUNTING, PLACE VALUE

GOALS:

- Multiply by 2
- Add to 19
- Develop understanding of place value

Meets NCTM Standards 2, 3, 4, 6, 7, 8 and 13.

MATERIALS:

- Base ten number blocks *or*
- Base ten Fun Money (p. 101)
- Two dice
- Recording Sheets for each player (p. 102)
- Pencils for each player

There are two blackline masters for this game. Fun Money (page 101) can be used if base ten blocks are unavailable. Fun Money comes in units (cents), tens (dimes) and hundreds (dollars). Players may enjoy coloring all the units one color, all the tens another color and all the hundreds a third color. This will also make the money more easily identifiable.

Use of the Recording Sheet (page 102) is explained in How to Play the Game, Steps 5, 6, 9, 10 and 11.

For a simpler version of this game, see "Take It to the Bank" in the addition section, page 48. For a more advanced version of this game, see "Multiplying Money," page 68.

OVERVIEW

Players, in turn, roll the dice, add up the sum and multiply that by two to earn base ten blocks or Fun Money. Whenever a player earns ten of any kind of block, he turns them into the bank in exchange for one of the next larger block. Through this exchange process, players learn how the base ten counting system works. Players count their earnings after each turn and add their new earnings to their previous total. They also record their totals after each turn, writing the amount of each kind of block on their Recording Sheets. This counting, adding and recording helps players develop an understanding of place value.

HOW TO PLAY THE GAME

1. The leader plays the role of the banker and holds all the "money" (the blocks).

2. Each player earns blocks by rolling two dice, **adding** numbers shown on the dice, and **multiplying** that sum by two.

3. Mike rolls a 3 and a 2. He adds this together to get 5 and multiplies that by 2 to get 10.

4. If a player's sum is correct, he receives that amount in base ten number blocks. Mike is correct, so he earns 1 ten rod.

5. After each turn, players add up their number blocks and write the total on their Recording Sheet. The first column on the sheet is hundreds (dollars), the second column is tens (dimes) and the third column is units (pennies). Mike has 1 ten rod, so he writes a "1" in the second column.

6. By writing the amounts in the correct columns of the Recording Sheets, players begin to understand **place value.**

7. On each subsequent turn, players roll the dice, add up the sum and multiply that by two.

8. When a player has 10 of any block, he trades them to the bank for 1 of the next higher blocks.

For ten unit blocks, you get one ten rod.

9. After trading in, the player then counts his blocks and writes the new total on his Recording Sheet.

10. This exchange with the bank and use of the Recording Sheet helps players understand place value.

11. The Recording Sheets also allow players to turn their blocks in to the bank and stop playing at any time. The sheets will contain a record of their earnings for the next time they want to play.

MULTIPLYING MONEY

MULTIPLYING, ADDING, COUNTING, PLACE VALUE

GOALS:

- Multiply by 1
- Multiply by 10
- Add up to 1000
- Further understanding of place value

Meets NCTM Standards 2, 4, 6, 7, 8 and 13.

MATERIALS:

- 1 set of base ten number blocks for each player OR
- 1 set of base ten Fun Money for each player (page 101)
- Pair (2) of dice
- Recording Sheets for each player (page 102)
- Pencils for each player
- 3 dice (Extension A)

There are two blackline masters for this game. Fun Money (page 101) can be used if base ten number blocks are unavailable. Fun Money comes in units (cents), tens (dimes) and hundreds (dollars). Players may enjoy coloring all the units one color, all the tens another color and all the hundreds a third color. This will also make the money more easily identifiable.

Use of the Recording Sheet (page 102) is explained in How to Play the Game, steps 7 and 9. For a slightly simpler version of this game, see "You Can Bank on It!," page 66.

OVERVIEW

Each player has a complete set of base ten number blocks or Fun Money, arranged in piles according to denomination. Players roll a pair of dice, multiply the lower number by ten and the higher number by one, and add these numbers. If they are

correct, they may take that amount from the base ten number blocks or Fun Money.

After each turn, players add to find their totals and write them down on the Recording Sheets. This helps players develop an understanding of place value. Whenever a player earns ten of any kind of block, he turns them into the bank in exchange for one of the next larger block. Through this exchange process, players learn how the base ten counting system works. The goal of the game is to earn the thousand cube.

In Extension A, players use a third die that represents hundreds, and are able to earn money more quickly. In Extension B, the leader sets a time limit for each turn; if players are not able to complete their roll and calculations within the time limit, they do not earn any blocks.

HOW TO PLAY THE GAME

1. Each player has a complete set of base ten number blocks or Fun Money. The blocks or Fun Money are arranged in piles according to amount: 1 thousand, 10 hundreds, 10 tens and 9 ones.

2. Players roll a pair of dice.

3. They **multiply** the die with the lower number by 10 and multiply the die with the higher number by 1. If both dice are the same number (for example, two 3s), players multiply one die by 10 and the other die by 1.

4. Luis rolls a 4 and a 6. He multiplies 4 by 10 to equal 40, and then multiplies 6 by 1 to equal 6.

5. If the sum is correct, players may take that amount from the number blocks or Fun Money in front of them. If the sum is not correct, they may not take any blocks or Fun Money.

6. Players must take the money in its proper form. Luis's total is 46, so he takes 4 ten rods and 6 unit blocks.

7. After each turn, players **add** their totals and write them down on their Recording Sheets. The first column in the sheets is hundreds, the second column is tens and the third column is units. Luis writes 4 in the tens column and 6 in the units column. This helps players with **place value.**

8. When a player has 10 of any kind of block, she trades them in for 1 of the next higher block. Luis eventually ends up with 11 ten rods and 9 unit blocks, so she trades in 10 of his ten rods for 1 hundred flat.

9. On his Recording Sheet, he writes "1" in the hundreds column, "1" in the tens column and "9" in the units column. Again, this trading in and recording helps her understand place value.

10. The goal of the game is to earn the thousand cube.

EXTENSIONS

A. Players who have been very successful with "You Can Bank on It!" (page 66) may play with 3 dice. The third dice should be taped so it only shows 1, 2, or 3. This die will tell players how many hundreds flats they have earned. They multiply the hundreds die by 1, and the other two die as in Step 3 above. Players accumulate money more quickly in this extension.

B. The leader sets a time limit of 20 seconds or less for each roll and calculations. If players cannot complete the roll and calculations within the time limit, they do not earn blocks.

SHARING SNACKS

DIVIDING, COUNTING

GOALS:

- Divide by numbers up to 5

Meets NCTM Standards 1, 2, 3, 4, 6, 7, 8 and 13.

MATERIALS:

- 15 raisins per player
- A higher number of raisins per player (Extension A)

Note: If food items are not appropriate in your classroom, this game may be played using blocks, beads, shells, etc. as counters.

OVERVIEW

The leader sets out a certain number of raisins and asks players to divide them evenly among themselves. The game starts out with one raisin per player and works up to five per player. In Extension A, the numbers of raisins varies, giving players practice dividing by a certain number they may find more challenging.

HOW TO PLAY THE GAME

1. The leader sets out as many raisins or counters as there are are players (for example, 4 raisins for 4 players).

2. The leader asks, "How many raisins do each of you get if you share the raisins equally?"

3. Players must **divide** the number of raisins by the number of players.

4. When they give the correct answer, each player gets 1 raisin.

5. The leaders next sets out twice the number of raisins as there are players 8 raisins for 4 players).

6. Repeat the question in Step 2.

7. Players again divide the raisins by the number of players.

8. The game continues for several rounds. At each round the number of raisins is increased.

EXTENSION

A. This is a good extension if players are having trouble dividing by 3, 4, 5, or even 6. Many players benefit from applying the same process of division with different low numbers. If there are three players, they can discover how to divide 9, 12, or 15 raisins. Four players, can divide 12, 16, or even 20. Five can divide 15, 20, or 25, and six can divide 18, 24, or 30 raisins.

Two for you and two for

LEADER'S NOTES

TWIN TOWERS

DIVIDING, COUNTING

GOALS:

- Divide 18 by 2, 3, 6 and 9
- Divide 2 into numbers up to 24 (Extension A)

Meets NCTM Standards 1, 2, 4, 6, 7, 8, 9, 10 and 13.

MATERIALS:

- 18 building blocks per player
- 24 Unifix® or other building blocks per player (Extension A)

Note: for a simpler version of this game, see "Towers of Power" in the Counting section, page 20.

OVERVIEW

Players are each given eighteen blocks. They first build two towers of equal height. The towers are to be built as tall as possible, block on block.

To do this, they have to divide their blocks evenly and count the blocks on their completed towers to make sure the towers are the same height.

They then break down their towers and build three towers of the equal height. Again, players must divide their blocks into even groups and count the heights of their towers after completion. This continues until players build nine towers of equal height.

In Extension A, players have twenty-four blocks and build two to twelve towers with the blocks, dividing up their blocks for each new tower.

HOW TO PLAY THE GAME

1. The leader gives each player 18 building blocks.

2. Players build 2 towers of the same height.

3. To do this, players must **divide** their eighteen blocks into 2 sets of 9 blocks each.

4. As they build the towers, players **count** the number of blocks each tower is made out of, confirming that they divided correctly.

5. At the end of this round, players break down their towers.

6. They next build 3 towers of the same height. To do so, players divide their blocks into 3 sets of 6 blocks each.

7. Once the towers are built, players again count the number of blocks in each tower, again confirming their division.

8. As the game continues, players build 6 and then 9 towers of the same height, dividing and counting their blocks at each round.

EXTENSION

A. Players are given 24 blocks. They divide their blocks and build 2, 3, 4, 6, 8 and 12 towers of equal height, counting the number of blocks in each tower at each round to confirm their division.

LEADER'S NOTES

FAMILY TRIP

DIVIDING, GROUPING

GOALS:

- Divide 8 by 2
- Divide 9 by 3

MATERIALS:

- 3 blocks of one color
- 9 blocks of a different color

Meets NCTM Standards 1, 2, 3, 4, 6, 7, 8 and 13.

OVERVIEW

Players start with two blocks representing parents and eight blocks representing children. The leader tells a story about a mother going on a business trip, taking some children with her. The other children stay at home with their father.

Players are told that the same number of children stay home as go on the trip, and must divide the eight blocks by two to find the answer.

In the next round, there are nine children, two parents and an aunt. An equal number of children go with one parent, or stay home with the other parent, or visit their aunt.

Players must divide the nine blocks by three to find the answer. This concrete representation helps players build a greater understanding of the process of division.

HOW TO PLAY THE GAME

1. The leader sets out 2 blocks of one color, say red, and 8 blocks of another color, say blue, and explains that the red blocks are parents and the blue blocks are their children.

2. The leader begins a story. Mr. and Mrs. Mumple have eight children. Mrs. Mumple goes away on a business trip, taking some of the children with her. An equal number of children stay at home with Mr. Mumple.

3. The leader asks, "How many children go away with Mrs. Mumple? How many stay home with Mr. Mumple?"

4. Players use the colored blocks to **divide** the children into 2 equal groups. Each red block should be grouped with 4 blue blocks.

5. Luis gives the correct answer, "Four children go with Mrs. Mumple and four children stay at home with Mr. Mumple."

6. The leader now puts out one more red block and one more blue block.

7. The story continues. The following year, the Mumples had a new baby. Mrs. Mumple, the baby, and some of the other children went to visit their grandparents. Some children stayed at home with Mr. Mumple and some children went to visit their Aunt Minnie instead. There are an equal number of children with Mrs. Mumple, Mr. Mumple, and their aunt, Minnie Mumple.

8. The leader asks, "How many children, including the baby, went away with Mrs. Mumple? How many stayed home with Mr. Mumple? How many went to visit their Aunt Minnie?"

9. Players again use the colored blocks to divide the children and the adults. Each red block should be grouped with three blue blocks.

10. Luis gives the correct answer, "Three children went with Mrs. Mumple, three children stayed at home and three children went off to visit Aunt Minnie."

LEADER'S NOTES

NUMBER CARDS

World Teachers Press®

World Teachers Press®

15

16

MAKING TRACKS

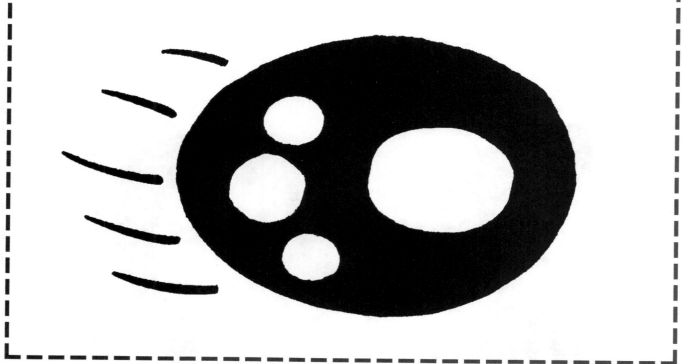

INSTRUCTIONS:

Copy this page five times. Then cut out the blocks to make 10 bear tracks. Arrange the bear tracks in a line for the children to count off when playing Making Tracks.

World Teachers Press®

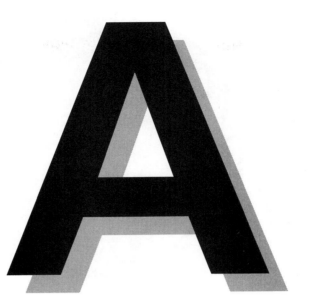

World Teachers Press®

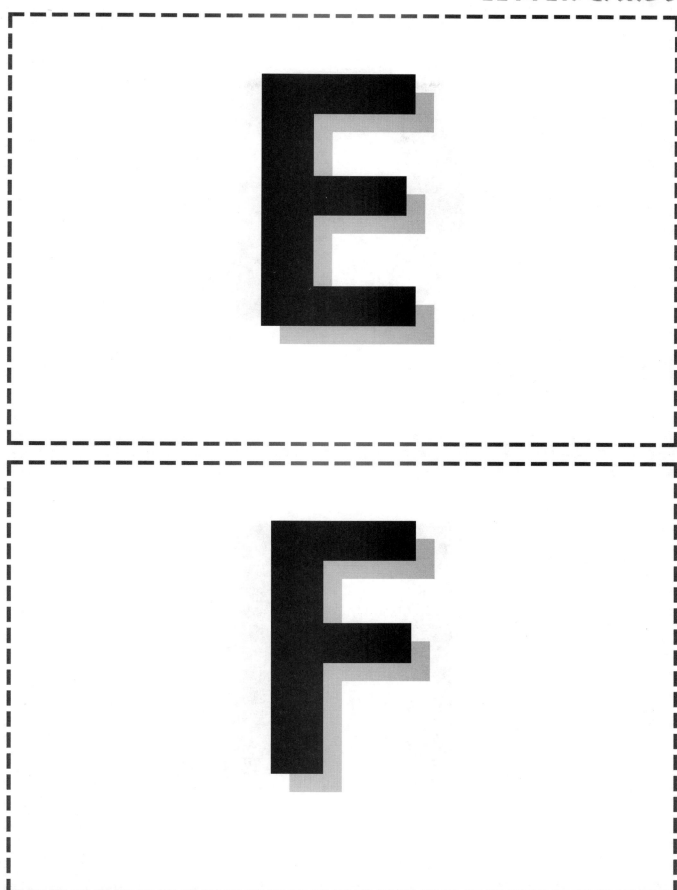

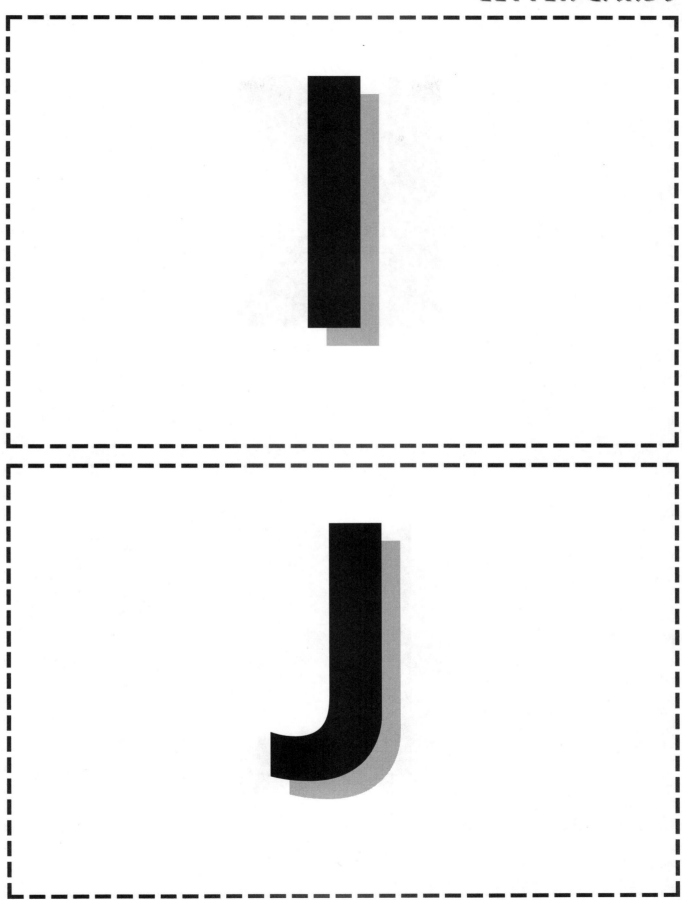

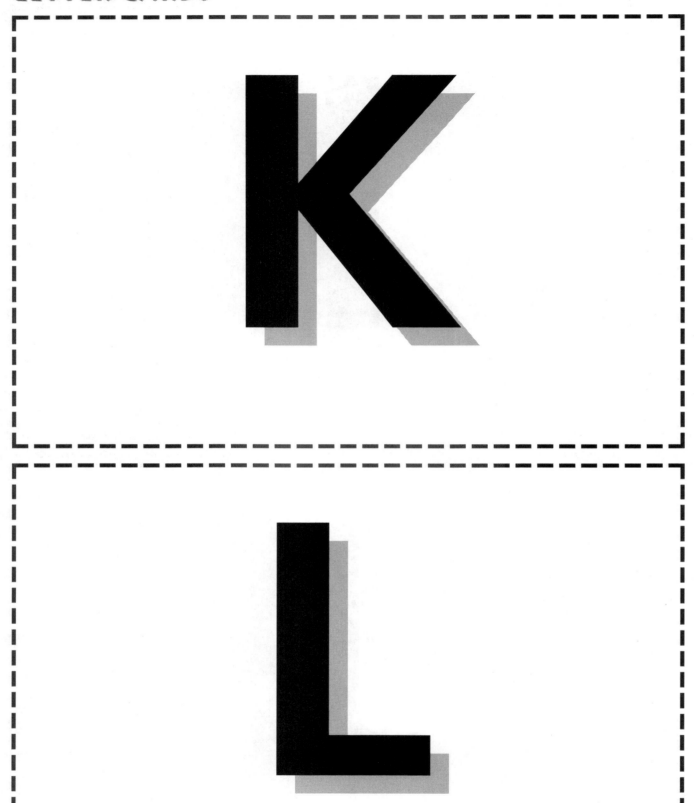

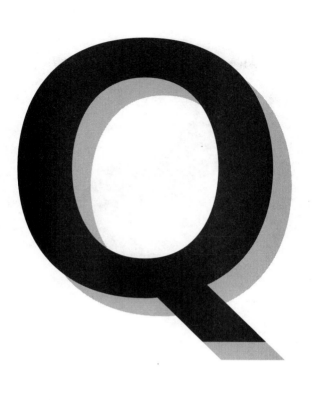

INSTRUCTIONS:

Cut the sheet into blocks and distribute an equal number to each player. Each player then colors the finger puppets and cuts them out along the dotted lines. Then the leader tapes the ends of the tabs together and fits them on to her fingers to play Birds of a Feather!

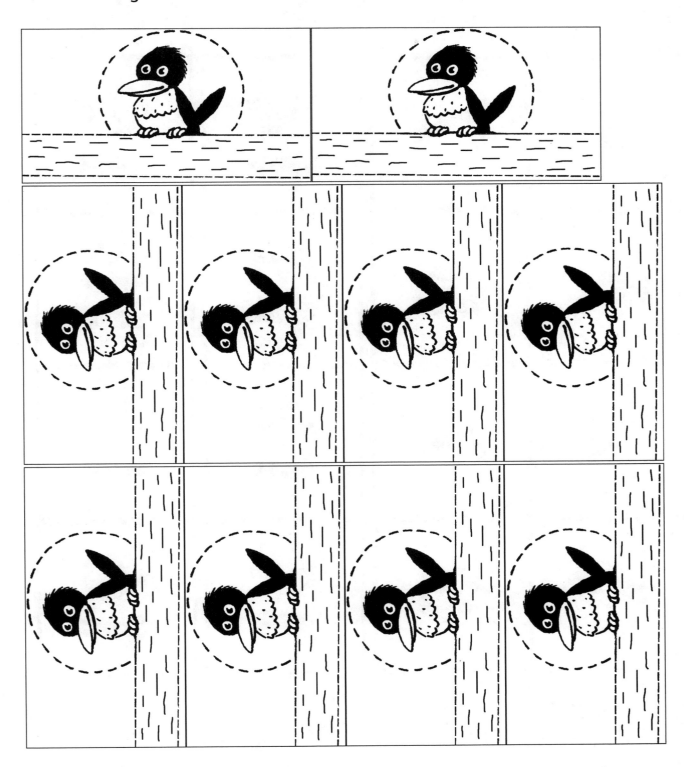

NUMBER LINE

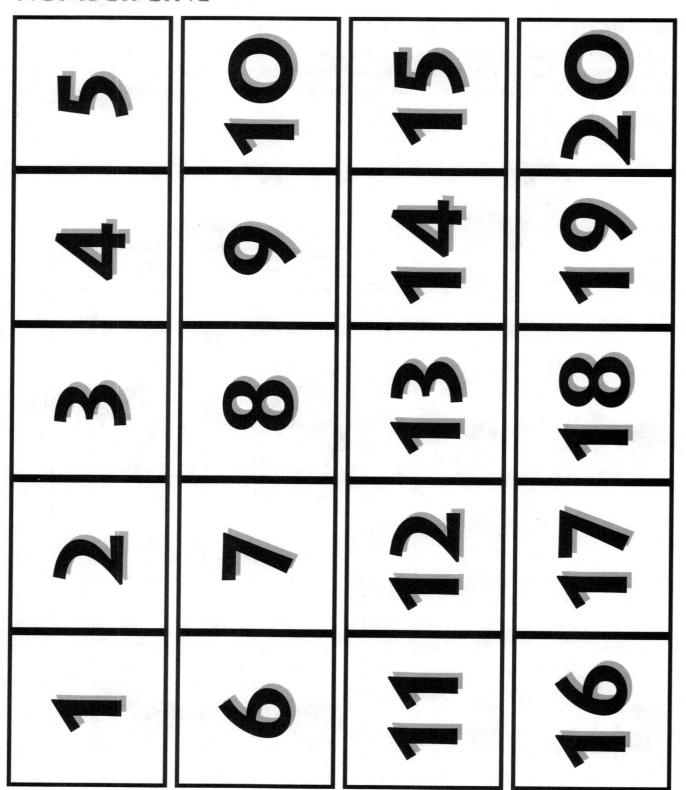

5	10	15	20
4	9	14	19
3	8	13	18
2	7	12	17
1	6	11	16

INSTRUCTIONS:

Cut numbers into strips (1 to 5, 6 to 10, 11 to 15, and 16 to 20). Then paste the strips together to form a number line from 1 to 10 or 1 to 20. See also next page for additional black line masters for The Archer and Backwards Numbers.

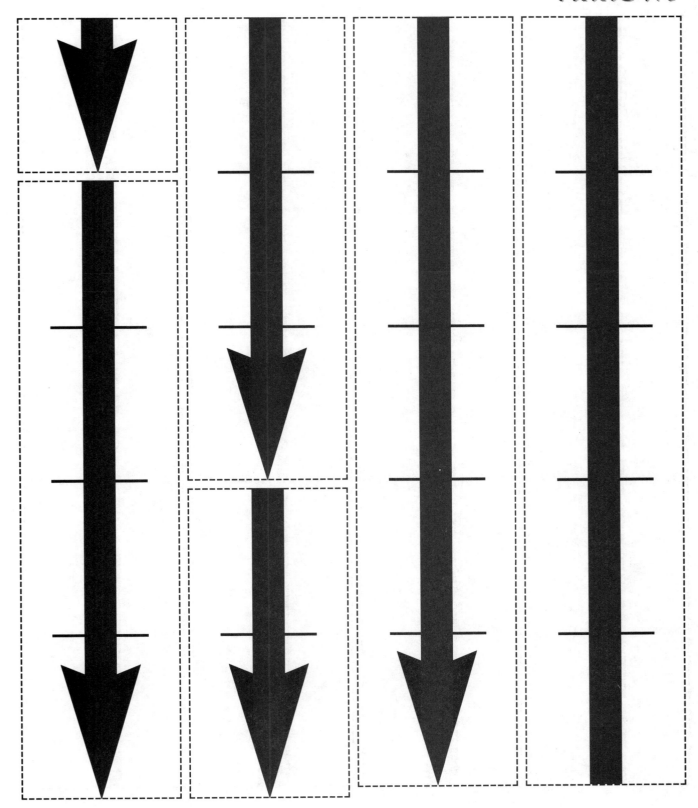

INSTRUCTIONS:

Cut out these arrows for The Archer and Backwards Numbers. You can create additional arrows ranging in length from 6 to 20 blocks by making photocopies and then combining the various length arrow heads with the shafts.

ARROWS

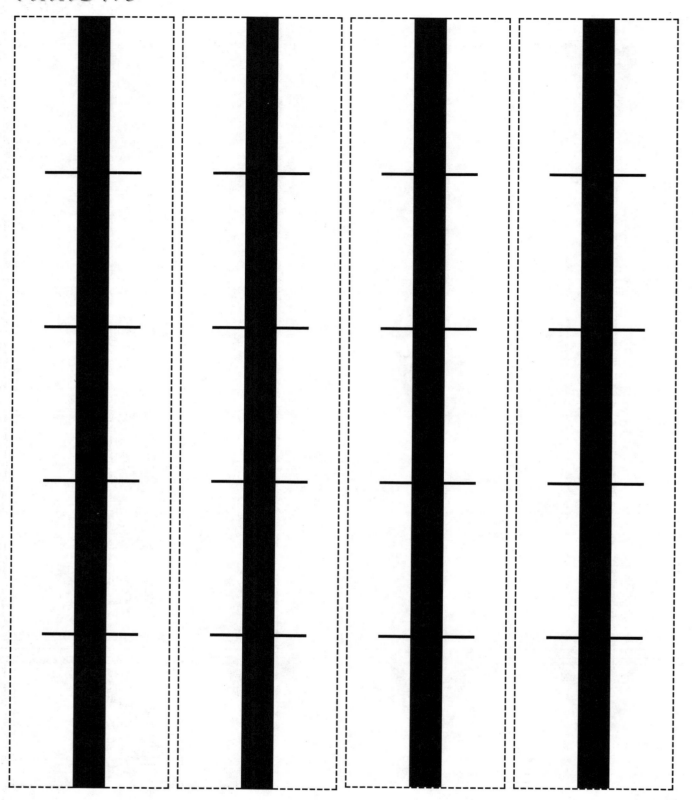

1¢	**1¢**	**1¢**
1¢	**1¢**	**1¢**
1¢	**1¢**	**1¢**
1¢	**10¢**	**10¢**
10¢	**10¢**	**10¢**
10¢	**10¢**	**10¢**
10¢	**10¢**	**$1.00**

RECORDING SHEET

Name:				Date:	
a.					
b.					
c.					
d.					
e.					
f.					
g.					
h.					
i.					
j.					
k.					
l.					
m.					
n.					
o.					
p.					
q.					
r.					
s.					
t.					
u.					
v.					
w.					
x.					
y.					
z.					

World Teachers Press®

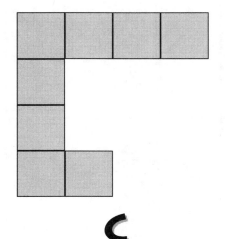

A

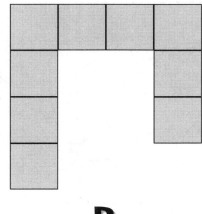

B

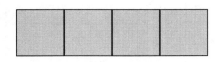

C

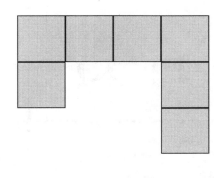

D

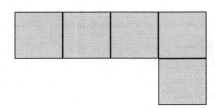

E

F

SHEEP IN A STORM

INSTRUCTIONS: Cut the sheet into blocks and distribute an equal number to each player. Each player then colors the sheep and cuts them out along the dotted lines. Next, they glue a soft cotton ball onto the circle inside each sheep to make 12 three-dimensional sheep for playing Sheep in a Storm!